Be who God meant you to be and you will set the world on fire.
— St. Catherine of Siena

Being GAY saved my life
The Art of Moving from Fear to Love

Manuscript, original art and book design by:
Diane Koziol Krueger

Edited by: Rosemary Sneeringer @
www.thebooknurturer.com

Being GAY saved my life
The Art of Moving from Fear to Love

For everyone who needs to know it's okay to be who you are.

SACRED

Transposed

Introduction
My Story

My story is purposefully spare and to the point.
I've written it down to get the stories out of my head and
because I believe my story will inspire some readers to
make choices that are right for them. This is not a tale of
doom and gloom. It's an illustration of my circumstances
and my choice to persevere with joy instead of despair.
To move from fear of everything, including myself,
to love of life and self.

Everyone is beautiful.

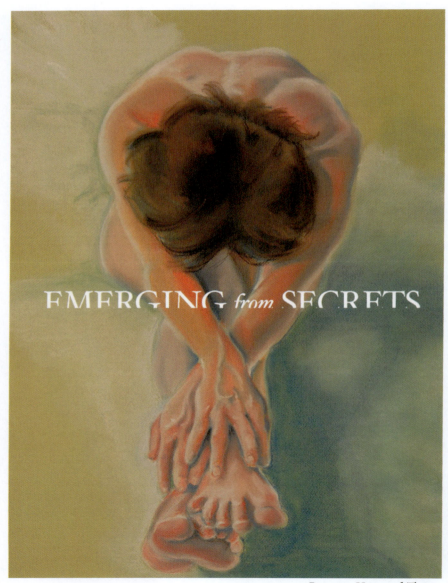

EMERGING *from* SECRETS

Between Here and There

Chapter I
On purpose

I don't blame my parents. Nothing is ever anyone's fault, life is just a series of choices. They provided a better environment for me than the ones they endured in their own childhoods. But a human being needs more than food, clothing and shelter to be truly alive.

I was born on February 25, 1965. My mom conceived me while she was on the pill. I arrived on a record snowstorm day, showing up a week early. From this, I can only conclude that I must have some purpose for being here.

I didn't always feel this way. Since I'm a product of a pill that skipped quality control, I was often introduced as an accident. I believed this. It's hard to develop a sense of self-worth when you are given the title of "Accident."

I've heard the theory that you pick your family and your role on this earth before you even arrive. Recently, I asked myself why I was born into this group of emotionally starved adults and why was I given the extra added bonus of being gay. I became part of a family with three siblings who were ten or more years older than me. They were young adults by the time I was five. I was surrounded by five other love-starved people. It was a household where it wasn't good to be seen OR heard. Don't make waves. Don't be different. I wasn't afraid to be different, I was afraid "to be."

The negative was always highlighted, never the positive. "Why did you do that?" "Why did you say that?" "What were you thinking?" Rarely a balancing positive statement was heard.

If I was upset about something, I was sent to my room to cry and could only come out when I was done. Nobody wanted to see emotion or acknowledge it. Out of sight, out of mind! I can still picture myself sitting in my bedroom, where I always sat when I cried: behind the door, on the floor, in a corner—and in front of a mirror. I don't really know why I chose to sit in front of a mirror because my other nicknames besides "The Accident" were: "Fats" and "Jane Swinia" (swinia is the Polish word for pig). I believed them. It was also drilled into me, during these formative years, that I had the "Koziol Nose" and the "Koziol (singing) Voice". This translated to BIG and BAD.

I have three children of my own and can't even imagine filling their heads with a constant barrage of negativity. How would they survive and become happy, healthy adults? How DID I survive without turning to drugs, alcohol or suicide?

How did I survive? By shutting down at an early age. Looking back, I'm sure by the time I was three I knew it wasn't safe to express myself or ask for what I needed.

As a toddler, I became a people-pleaser and continued this until only a few years ago.

How did being gay save my life? Being born gay is like an automatic placement into a special-interest group. That special interest is self-love. It's as if I was given a built-in mechanism to initiate my self-love process through the challenges of peer pressure and conditional love prevalent in our society. Being gay calls upon all the personal fortitude you have to accept yourself just as you are. And that acceptance becomes the catalyst for unconditional love—unconditional love for yourself and people you meet along the way.

Being gay also got me to a therapist because I thought this was the main issue I needed to address in my life. Fortunately, my brilliantly kind therapist taught me so much more and helped me heal from the real issues of emotional abandonment. Only recently can I look at myself in a mirror and love who I am. My story isn't about all things sad. It is about healing and happiness—that we all have choices and that those choices belong to us.

My Sister

My sister always wants kisses. But I do not want to give her one, Because I do not like them. She is 20 years old. her name is Barb

Koziol Diane

Chapter 2
The house I grew up in

I thought about calling this chapter the home I grew up in but the term "home" would be over-promising. There were six of us in a small-sized cookie-cutter house built in the 1950's. It was one of those neighborhoods where, from an aerial view, every house looked identical. Since on the outside all the houses looked alike, as a child, I assumed they were identical on the inside as well. They were all the same when it came to floor plans, but now I realize each had their own set of emotional plans.

I was the youngest of four children. I was ten years younger than my youngest sibling. They were all a year or two apart from each other. The oldest is my sister and quite possibly my nemesis. She was entering her teenage years when my cute baby self was brought on the scene, rivaling her for what little positive emotional attention my parents were doling out. We were—and are—total opposites.

She's girly, frilly and loves dolls. I'm feminine, but I prefer my clothing to be lace and peplum-free. I'm athletic, gravitate toward cowboy boots (I'm butch from the ankles down) and took comfort in stuffed animals instead of dolls. My sister didn't just love dolls, she was and is still obsessed with them. Looking back, I believe she tried to make me one of her dolls, and, worse yet, give the attention that she wanted and needed from my parents to me. This was not the attention I needed.

I didn't want to be dressed in chiffon party dresses pushing around a hard plastic baby doll in a toy stroller. She wanted all that.

And she wanted love. I remember often having to "pay" for some desirable toy or playtime with her with kisses. I could have whatever it was . . . for a kiss.

I believe that my love, whether in the form of kisses or humor or making them feel good about themselves, became some sort of payment for their attention. I even wrote an "essay" in second grade called "My Sister." I still have the original document that reflects my theory:

My sister always wants kisses. But I do not want to give her one, because I do not like them. She is twenty years old. Her name is Barb.

As far as my oldest brother goes, I don't remember much. He had moved out of the house by the time I was in second or third grade. He didn't come around often and moved to another state in his twenties, making only obligatory phone calls to my parents and flying in for Christmas. There is no judgment here, just observation.

I didn't see a reason to connect with my family of origin either that doesn't come with, "Well, I suppose I SHOULD call." Should—the real "S" word. I can only hope my kids are motivated to call and visit when they are grown and out of the house from an authentic place of wanting to connect and not from a place of "should." I believe they already know that their company is ENJOYED by me and their father.

My other brother is ten years older than me. During his mid-twenties he was diagnosed as a paranoid schizophrenic. Before this, I remember him as the liveliest of the sibs. He was the one who always liked to initiate conversation at family gatherings—often taking a stand and turning a conversation into a debate for the sake of arguing. Maybe it was for the sake of some emotional energy and sharing of opinions within the family. Overall, it didn't go over well, because no one wanted controversy or conflict. Silence was better because you could keep your feelings to yourself and not have to see or hear anyone else's.

My dad. He went to work. Came home. Read the paper. Ate dinner. Watched the news and sitcoms du jour until he went to bed. Not a man of fun energy. He did play catch, ping-pong and pool with me and paid for my college education (my sister paid a portion too). I never saw him really happy. The only life-ism he gave me happened in junior high. He looked at me and said, "Life isn't fun." I believed him.

Also, it wasn't a good idea to leave the street without permission or play with matches. I know, because I was caught doing both—for which I was spanked by him in a fit of rage. This, I guess, was to let me know I did something wrong, but no one ever explained the dangers of leaving the street at a very young age or why we don't play with matches.

My father passed away recently and while clearing out his belongings from the house, I came across his drumsticks. I had forgotten my father was in a band before he was married. It made me wonder: What happens to make people leave their passions behind or forget them altogether? Why did it take me so long to return to drawing and creating? Why did my father never pick up those drumsticks again? Did we both feel unworthy of enjoyment in our lives?

My mom. She had a long daily to-do list living in an era of woman-folk work. She did everything—cooking, cleaning, scheduling, buying school supplies . . .
It always seemed to be her goal to get these things "over with" on a daily basis so she could read her magazines. She was almost always home, but she wasn't truly there.

I remember my senior year in high school being devastated because I wasn't asked to prom. Being gay, there wasn't any boy I really wanted to go with, but rejection is rejection. Prom was on a Saturday night, and because I attended a Catholic School, the Prom opening event was mass—the regular Saturday night mass we always went to. Of course, on this evening I didn't want to go. I never told my mom why, so she made me go. She didn't even know it was Prom night.

So, while all my friends walked into church with their dates, I sat between my parents. After mass, my mom tried to comfort me by putting her arm around me and telling me some sad dating story of hers. Having taken care of myself emotionally for eighteen years, I hated feeling my mother's arm around me. I hated her touch. Touch of any kind was foreign to me and made me uncomfortable.

Many years later, my mom told me of a senior citizens' event she was planning to attend and asked if she could borrow my (non-existent) prom dress.

The Final Family Member—the TV

The TV was always on in my parent's house. The first person awake turned it on. The last person to bed turned it off. Most of the laughter in the house came from sitcom laugh tracks. Up until his death, my dad still ate his meals at the kitchen table with a radio right next to him that had a TV tuner. He could listen to the news or game shows without having to be reminded that a real story was going on right in front of him. His chair even faced the TV in the other room, instead of anyone else at the table.

I have no memories of sharing of current events during dinnertime. Eating was all function.

Chapter 3
Early drawing

Early on, I figured out how to use what I had. One way I discovered to get attention was through my drawings. I've always loved Snoopy. I can't even remember when I was originally drawn to Snoopy, but I do recall sitting down with a stack of paper, a pencil and my Peanuts® pillowcase around the time I was in second grade. I drew him over and over and over again until it looked "just like" Charles Schultz's rendering. I believe it was perfect. To this day, childhood friends connect drawings of Snoopy to their memories of me.

Looking back and analyzing everything, I can see how a good drawing got me positive attention. Positive words were even said out loud. These words were for me—for my ears to take in. I could hold up a "perfect" drawing and hear words like "good" and "nice" being directed right at me.

Even as an adult I would read the Peanuts comic strip and

collect all things Snoopy. I still have my original Snoopy; my son is now his caretaker. After a couple of years of weekly therapy, I came to realize how smart Charles Schultz's words "Good Grief" are. In my therapy sessions, I would experience crying that my therapist would call "joy pain." Joy pain is moving through an issue instead of around it. Joy pain is healing instead of harboring. It's looking at an experience and saying: "Yes that hurt," and "Yes it wasn't good for me," but I survived and I can now make other choices for myself. It's realizing that you have a right to be happy and be loved no matter how your past played out. And, of course, it's important to acknowledge and not blame. As adults, we can choose love and happiness, to give it freely AND RECEIVE it back, and to know we deserve it.

I got so accustomed to this "Good Grief" crying that I told my therapist if I didn't cry in a session, I didn't feel I was getting my money's worth! She laughed. She knew it was true—she knows the value of healthy crying.

In the beginning days of therapy, when I would start to sob, my therapist was saying something to me I don't think I heard until after a few crying sessions. She was saying, "Make a sound." I had to think for a moment, "What did she mean?" Then it dawned on me—my crying was silent. I had mastered releasing even the most back-heaving sobs in complete silence. My life had taught me to keep my emotions to myself because they may upset someone else. To this day, I'm still working on this one. When one thing or another has made me cry, which I now recognize as good, I tell myself, "Make a sound." And then I listen for my voice.

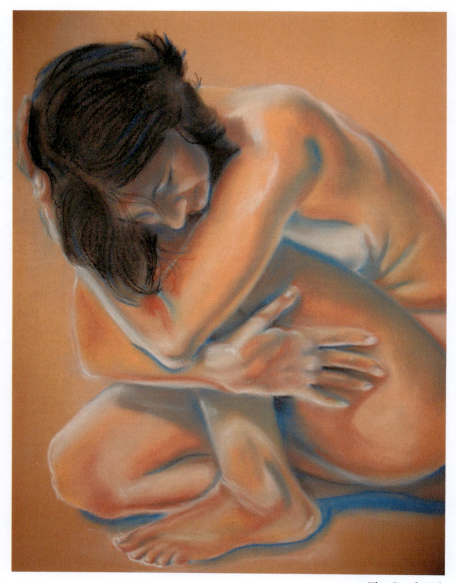

The Good Girl

Chapter 4
Catholic School

Twelve years of Catholic school.

My therapist had the best response to that statement. She said, "My condolences."

For me, Catholic school in the 70's and 80's was just another non-nurturing environment. I would leave my home, where self-expression wasn't allowed, and go off to the exact same environment with adults who were just as angry "looking after" me.

I remember in the fourth grade, a group of us—mostly girls for some reason—received "Little Progress" on our report cards, in the worst possible subject in a parochial school. This mothership equivalent of an F+ was in RELIGION. Holy-Holy Shit!

A group of us was sent down to see Holy Mother Sister Principal. Her mission was to scare us. She threatened to send all of us back to second grade for a semester AND tell our parents. I was ten. I believed her. I'm not sure which I thought was worse. Going back two years of my life was inconceivable to me and stunned me into panic. I began to sob uncontrollably along with almost the rest of the group. I say "almost" because one girl stood her ground and wouldn't give it up. She wouldn't choose the emotion Sister Mary Fuck With Your Head wanted from us. Sister MFWYH even called her out of the group and asked, "What's the matter with you?! Why aren't you crying?!" The principal was sooo angry at this ten-year-old girl, her face was hell-fire red.

Well, it was a scare tactic and no one was sent back to second grade. And if you're wondering why I got this low mark in religion class, it was because I forgot to have a certain page of homework signed by my parents, which prevented me from turning in all the rest of my A+ work that WAS completed. (I was too scared not to do A+ work and get good grades.) Since that paper wasn't signed, everything else was disallowed.

So yet another unhealthy environment I was placed in and survived. But wouldn't it have been great to have the personal fortitude of the girl who wouldn't allow herself to be manipulated by this unloving adult?

I tell my own children that hearing something from an adult doesn't automatically make it right or true.

Chapter 5
The Girl Scout story

I hate camping. I'm probably the only lesbian who doesn't own a tent. I'm not a princess. I'm only high maintenance when it comes to accommodations. I can play in nature from sunrise to sunset, but at the end of the day, please drive me back to the resort.

Maybe I don't like camping because of a Girl Scout experience the summer before sixth grade.

For two weeks of camp, we were provided with tents that were slightly deluxe. They were assembled of canvas AND screens on wooden platforms a couple of feet off the ground. As palatial as these were, we were still in the woods—meaning bugs and vermin. One of the rules was: "No candy in your tent!" My friends and I were only ten or eleven years old, so this rule was never followed.

One night, returning to our tent after a day of trefoil activities, we heard a squeaking sound. We stood quietly, trying to trace its source. At first we thought and hoped it was someone's fashionable metal belt buckle—it WAS the seventies—until we noticed the movement in the sleeping bag—MY sleeping bag! Well, the first thing the four of us eleven year olds thought to do (simultaneously) was SCREAM. The counselors came to our tent, unhappy with our paging system, but they helped me anyway. They took my sleeping bag outside the tent and unzipped it to find a mother mouse and several freshly born pink babies clinging to the blanket inside. To this day, I am grateful for all their squeaking, which prevented me from curling up with the new family that night.

Why am I sharing this story with you? Well, even after the mouse family was relocated, I didn't want to use my sleeping bag. And none of us wanted to sleep in our tent until daylight proved it was sans mice. So we roomed with the girls in the next tent. Eight of us in a four-person tent.

By the middle of the night, with no sleeping bag that I wanted to use, I was very cold. Another girl noticed I was awake and shivering. She told me to get in her sleeping bag with her. (No, there is no gay twist to this story.) She held me and kept me warm and even said something out loud about how badly I was shaking and how cold I felt. I had never experienced this kind of compassion before. I was raised in a place of "be glad for what you got" and don't ask for more. This little girl was African American and the only thing my fourth grade mind could conclude was, "Oh, black families must be different." Different in a good, helpful, kind and compassionate way, but those words weren't in my head back then.

When I told my therapist this story a few years ago, she said two things:

1. "That was a beautiful story," and 2. "Why didn't you ask the counselors for a blanket?" At 43, I had no answer for her. I had no idea that it was okay to ask for what I needed. I didn't even know it was an option. She told me some kids would have had demanded immediate action— a blanket or a phone call home to their parents. None of that occurred to me then or later as I stared blankly back at my therapist.

I don't remember this girl's name. The summer camp was composed of girls from all over the Detroit area and she wasn't from my original troop. But I will always be grateful to her and her kind actions. After my therapy appointment that day, I sent out a thank you to that little girl and trusted the Universe to take it to her.

Everybody Else's Girl

Chapter 6
The Marriage

I would never let myself say the G word—not even in my head. I didn't want to be gay. I prayed to God to undo it. Let me be like everyone else. Although, after all this personal growth, I understand there is no "like everyone else."

I always wanted to be a mom, have a family and go to Disney World. I wanted to experience pregnancy and childbirth too. Well, I've done all those things. I have three beautiful children and we've been to Disney World more than once. We even claim our right of parenting passage with our I've-Been-To-Disney Mickey head antenna toppers.

Having given birth to three fabulous children, I have no regrets. Being a mom has never been a false mask, and, at the time, I couldn't see how to have a family any other way besides being the quintessential society-approving way.

I became the quintessential hero child from my upbringing —having kids AFTER getting married to a MAN they approved of. (They didn't ask for this approval, I was looking for it.) Setting up a Lesbian two-mommy household would be opposite of a society-approving lifestyle. My family didn't expect me or urge me to have babies or get married. It was in my head to do it this way in order to gain other people's approval.

I also believe that these three kids not only chose their mission here on earth, but also banded together pre-birth out in the Universe and decided to take this trip together!

Like straight girls in their late twenties, I started to pick up the pace on a partner hunt. I set out to find someone. I found my co-parent through video dating. Out of the wall of endless tapes and profiles, we picked each other. This relationship was meant to be. Not in the "till death do us part" way. But certainly in a growing-through-crisis way. One of my favorite sayings is "don't let a good crisis go to waste." It's true. When realizing that divorce was inevitable, my former spouse put it best, "We both got into a relationship where it was okay not to share all of our feelings."

We dated for a few years, got married, and since I was already in my thirties and we both wanted more than one child, I got pregnant after the first year of marriage. I decided I wanted to be a stay-at-home mom and left my professional career and life. I wouldn't do that again. While it was great for the kids and it made my spouse's schedule very easy, I recommend keeping one foot in the door of some kind of income source for anyone entering into marriage and parenting. Our three children are two years apart in age, so this kept me busy mentally, physically and emotionally for the first five years or so.

There wasn't really time to think about me.
During the course of the marriage I slowly gave up all my power. Not having any knowledge of personal growth, and not wanting to disappoint, I gave in to everything. He would tell you decisions were 50/50, but they weren't. I couldn't stand up for myself to oppose an idea he had. As soon as I saw the first facial expression of disapproval from him I would give in. It became a parent/ child relationship or an authoritarian/subservient one. He would disagree on this view of things but I can look back and see how giving up my power gave him the power to create an illusion of choice.

"We" bought his parents' house, which was, to me, an unappealing fixer-upper. We had a two year old and a second child arriving in a month. So I ended up living in a house I never wanted, purchased with an un-smart financing plan, and moving in with my new constant companions: My in-laws.

My in-laws are not bad people. In fact, I've had more one-on-one interesting and respectful conversations with my mother-in-law than my former spouse. No, it wasn't ALL bad living together, but I can't imagine many wives sending up a special prayer asking, "Dear God, please let me live, for a considerable length of time, with my in-laws at some point in my marriage."

The plan included living with his parents for a few months until his dad's retirement came through. His dad was old-fashioned and even drew up a living-together contract with terms that stated when my father-in-law was in charge and the date my spouse would take over and be in charge. According to his document, the women were never in charge. It did, however, come with an organized cooking schedule for my mother-in-law and myself!

I hated everything about this house. A friend who came to visit and see our new son commented, "It's so weird to see you in a place that's not you."

After my in-laws continued with their retirement plan and moved out, the remodeling plan proceeded by moving our daily living area—daily for me, a two year old and a new-born—to an area of the cobwebby, stucco-walled, peel-ing-floor-tiled unfinished basement. The thirty-year-old appliances and cupboards were relocated from the main floor kitchen to the basement. This was not a fancy walk out basement. This was a storage/laundry room kind of basement. Including the basement, the house was three stories. The middle, main living area was the renovation site. Our bedrooms were on the third floor. This did not make it easy for nap times and frequent diaper changes. I lived in the basement or upstairs in the also unfinished, well-worn bedroom level for a year and four months.

My former spouse still rolls his eyes at me with no sympathy or gratitude for this—to him it was no big deal. Well, he went to work or worked on the house. He didn't spend the time I did living in a construction zone with my in-laws. When it came time to divide up what little we had for the divorce mediation, who got the house was NEVER an issue. I left the structure happily!

More than once my babies got sick because his siblings thought it was okay to bring contagious children to family functions. After one of these events, I would end up stuck at home, with round-the-clock sick children and he would go to work. If I got sick along with them, he would get angry. Not an outward yelling anger, but more of an impatient being-inconvenienced anger that his schedule would have to be adjusted to help out at home. He gave me minimal support during these times, maybe coming home an hour early from work but never missing a team sport he was scheduled to play that night. He would throw me a bone by skipping the after-play bar time with his friends and come home to help. By then, we were usually asleep.

Family vacations were an issue too. Before marriage I took nice vacations—a hotel room and an interesting location. Or a visit to see my brother in Florida and stay IN a house and go outside to take in the sun!

My former husband came from a vacation mentality that was all about frugal and family. The family part was okay with me. I enjoyed most of his relatives and probably would have enjoyed them more at a larger facility.

On my video dating profile, I stated quite clearly that I don't like to camp. Maybe my former spouse chose to ignore this statement or he saw it as his duty to enlighten me to the joys of outdoor living.

There were two yearly reunion-like trips (I can't call them vacations) that were required. I say "required" because in later years, when I would want to negotiate shorter stays, his compromise was, "Well, don't go then." Even though I didn't want to go, his compromise was still hurtful.

These trips would usually last at least a week. Some lasted nine days. They involved 20-plus relatives, a musty cottage with one bathroom—yes ONE toilet—plenty of women-folk work AND sleeping in a tent. There used to be a rule that the family with the youngest child would get one of the two indoor rooms but that rule changed when one forceful relative no longer had the youngest child. She and her family moved out of state and changed the rule to "the family traveling the greatest distance gets the indoor accommodations." So we were "welcomed" to put our tent up in the backyard (for several days). Even with babies, we'd have the portable crib in the tent. Now all this would be fine if both people in the relationship agreed on the amount of time spent on a trip like this.

After the divorce, sharing my true dislike and details of these trips with married friends, their jaws would drop at what I agreed to. One said, "OMG I thought you liked those trips!" One of his relatives, knowing I hated them said, "Sometimes you have to sacrifice for family." Hmmmm. Compromise maybe. But sacrifice?

My former husband had an annual hunting trip, a custom started before I knew him. The trip would consist of at least nine days of being away in another state. This was fine with me until we started having children. It takes a lot of energy to be a single parent for nine days with toddlers and newborns. When I asked him to shorten his trips, he got angry and told me I SHOULD know how important this was to him and do whatever necessary to make them happen for him.

Hunting trips took place just before Thanksgiving. So I would also be planning and shopping for the Thanksgiving dinner I hosted and prepared for my side of the family. I must have created the illusion of not needing any help from them either, since none was offered. They would bring something to the dinner if I asked them to, but I would also have to help them decide what to bring.

So the husband would return home after spending a week in a tree with a gun hoping to be greeted by a wife who threw her arms around him and wanted "I've-been-away-for-a-week sex," regardless of how tired I was from doing it ALL for EVERYONE.

I look back on these years and take full responsibility for not being able to say no or ask for help, I also look back and wonder how I endured.

You may be wondering how a gay woman survives the sex life as an assumed hetero. During the marriage, his sex drive never diminished. I got married thinking it would wane after a while. I was wrong!   First of all, I believe you can have bad sex but I don't believe there is such a thing as a bad orgasm. And no, I never faked an orgasm. I'm a firm believer in vitamin O! Also, I find kissing and touching more intimate than the actual act of sex itself, so I did less and less of that as the years went on. It is also my opinion that men can view frequency as having a good sex life. My goal was fast and his was frequent.

I trained myself to shut down. Using what I learned as a toddler, I kept everyone else happy. After I came out, I realized I was having more sex than I desired, of course, AND more than my married hetero friends. Hiding is never healthy.

Now, I do believe in manifesting: asking the Universe for what you want and receiving it. I have to thank my former husband, who came home one day from work and shared with me a conversation-starting question he had asked of his staff: What one thing do you want to do before you die? Out loud, I answered him with, "I don't know." But in my head I said, "To be in a relationship that's right for ME." I know the Universe was listening because, looking back, this is my beginning of connecting the dots to my personal growth and returning to being me.

Rebirth

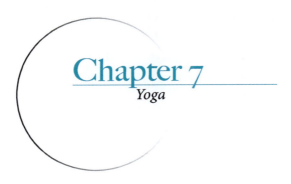

Chapter 7
Yoga

A few months later I found myself in a yoga class. I had recently been paying attention to things that occurred more than once around me. Leaving a cycling class one day, a fellow spinning friend said, "Have you ever tried yoga? I think you'd like it." I told him no, I've always been curious about it, and went into my "How would I work another thing into my workout schedule with three little kids?" speech. Not two minutes later, a friend stopped me in the locker room and said, "Have you ever tried yoga? I think you'd like it." And she proceeded to tell me what class and time she would be at, so I wouldn't have to try it by myself.

And I went! I loved it! I've never stopped going! I didn't even know what I loved about it, but I always looked forward to going. One of the best parts is I had no preconceived expectations of yoga. I had no idea about the power of going within or had ever heard of getting a yoga-butt! The only thing I knew was sitting crossed-legged and chanting "om," which isn't even a staple of my practice.

I would follow along and look around in yoga class trying to figure out all these new moves and poses with fun names like "down dog down" or "sit spot sit" (and wrap your ankles around your back while you're at it too).

Once I began stretching my body and lifting my heart to the sky, the many messages of love and self love began to penetrate my emotional armor.

And I began drawing again—signing up for a class that was a little longer of a drive and a little pricier than a local city class because I WAS WORTH IT!   Not computer-generated drawing, but two semesters of figure drawing. I've always loved the human form and ended up in the right classes with the right instructors. I reconnected to a left-behind passion of mine.

Yoga was also a catalyst for coming out. The studio where I practice yoga uses the theme "Free yourself to be yourself." Besides reconnecting me with my passion for art, the practice of yoga was allowing me to see me as me. I had never had a lesbian affair or date in reality. I knew how to lock my desires down. From adolescence until this point, I would fall asleep thinking about my "crush de jour" or de semaine or de mois.

I don't have gender issues but I would imagine myself as the faceless boyfriend of one these crushes. (Maybe I was a homophobe?) Now, instead I was seeing the reality of what could be. I could picture myself being a woman with a woman and being okay with it. This was a huge revelation for me. I think it brought me to the planet. My original plan for this secret of mine—the secret of being the G-word—was to take it to my grave and never experience what's right for me. Can you imagine holding all your natural God-given passions on the inside, letting it eat away at you until your hair starts to fall out? (Which mine was beginning to do.)

I say God-given here because sexuality is NOT a choice. Trust me. I spent the majority of my life trying to make it a choice, trying to force myself to be the way I thought society wanted me to be—attracted to people I couldn't be attracted to: Men.

So, as I'm experiencing trance states of yoga bliss, an instructor shares with us that after the initial bliss, yoga will pull the rug out from under your feet. Boy, was he right! I found myself drawn to take a yoga workshop. A workshop that would involve sharing and doing other uncomfortable things such as moving around freely in front of people. As much as I hated this, I was compelled to sign up. I sat in the circle, shared, and danced to drumbeats in the semi-darkness.

By the end, I was bunched up. My therapists loves that term "bunched up." She'll say, "Ooooh what's going on? You haven't used that term in awhile." She knows when something pushes me off balance. So there I was, bunched up and looking at everyone else in the room. They were hugging and laughing and feeling the love. I was ready to throw up!

Curious about all this and innately knowing I needed help, I emailed the yogi who led the class to ask her why I was not feeling the love. Why did I leave angry and nauseous? She read my e-mail and suggested I talk to her on the phone. Crap. I just wanted to have an impersonal e-mail solve my problem. But I called her. She asked me some questions about then and now. She said maybe something was coming up for me and gave me the name of my now-therapist. From other people's therapy horror stories, I can say that I was very fortunate to connect with a smart, helpful, compassionate not-let-you-get-away-with-any-crap therapist from the get-go.

Yes, something was coming up for me. More than I could even imagine. As I mentioned earlier, I thought the only issue in my life was my secret of being gay. Once I came out to her, which wasn't easy but was done quickly, we began healing why I wasn't okay with being myself and all the other growing-up patterns and beliefs I thought were true.

She gave me techniques to withstand the backlash of coming out and its effects on the people around me, but I can honestly say, my relationships with my friends only grew closer.

"Once we've reached out for love enough times and felt unloved in return, we shut down and try to defend ourselves against the blow we subconsciously have come to expect."

-Marianne Williamson
"The Gift of Change"

Rebirth

Unfoldin

Chapter 8
Coming out

From the time I came out to my husband until I started coming out to family members on an individual basis, my family could sense something wasn't right. The hero child was not herself. I came out to an adult niece first because she approached me in a compassionate human way with, "If you want to talk, I'm ready to listen." I found out later that she and her sister were worried I was dying of cancer.

On the other, "I-know-what-you-need without-asking-you" hand, my mom and sister, seeing that the hero child was no longer peppy and happy, making all the holiday dinners for the tenth year in a row, living with a controlling husband in an unfinished house with an old drape stapled to 2 x 4's to simulate a wall, they decided it must be menopause. They were even planning to present me with menopause survival book. I wasn't in menopause and didn't appreciate the diagnosis or the bestseller gift.

When I came out to my family of origin, I came out on two subjects. I came out about my sexuality and I came out of the old family patterns I wasn't going to play along with anymore. I believe they had no problem with the gay part because it took the focus off the unhealthy family pattern part. Some were ready to storm my therapist's office and give her a piece of their mind for helping me disturb the family way and for helping me feel my emotions and want to talk about them. I told them this was a great idea and offered my therapist's phone number so the whole fucking family could be healed. Yes I was angry — another emotion no one wanted to see. But I know from my own experience you have to be ready to allow the healing.

I've asked my siblings what was it like for them, growing up in Mom and Dad's house. That question alone made some of them angry with me and they DIDN'T want to admit anything was wrong with our upbringing. They said things like, "Sure Mom and Dad were strict but so were many of our friend's parents down the street." I let the subject go at this point. A few years earlier, BPG (before personal growth) I would have defended my childhood too. But just because "that's how it was" doesn't mean it was right, or that being raised in an environment lacking love has to continue.

One sibling who corroborated my feelings of fear and isolation (and has his own stories to share about his childhood) is the one who is a diagnosed paranoidschizo-phrenic. I wonder if my other siblings would discount his feelings too because of his mental illness. I know I used to. Thirty years ago when he was going through his own revealing crisis and mental illness diagnosis, I wanted him to just take his medication and rebury all this emotion he was stirring up in the family and go back to business as usual: No emotion. AND PLEASE stop making the rest of us SO uncomfortable. STOP MAKING ME FEEL!!

Recently, when I asked him what it was like living at home, he shared a "family happening" about me—one that I would have been too young to remember. (As a side note here, his mental illness prevents him from lying. He's always honest to the point of being insulting. If he doesn't like your hair or clothes he will gladly tell you. So if you're sporting a new 'do, beware! This is why I trust this story).

He recalled me as a toddler wearing my cute pajamas with the feet in them, and how I would go around to each family member at night, giving them kisses over and over again. He recalled it as a game. He described me as "The Love in the Family." What he saw as a cute family ritual, I see as a very sad picture of a child in the middle of a ring of robots trying to breathe some happy life into them.

When I came out to my mom, I told her I'm gay and getting a divorce. The first thing she said was, "You're brave." She pointed to her temples and then pointed off in space and continued to say, "I've seen people like this on Oprah, and they're much happier later."

I think my decision to do what's right for me resonated with her feeling trapped and stuck in her own marriage. My parents aren't bad people, they just never caught on to life skills to better their lives. It's my observation that they were each waiting for the other to be the catalyst for happiness. I remember growing up how often my mom would be at her wit's end and say, "I'm so sick and tired of staring at these same four walls!"

When I came out to my husband, it was a blow to him, but one of the first things he said was, "Well, some things make sense now." There were plenty of mean-spirited things said, such as, "It's your fault I wasn't a better husband." But for the most part we were able to move toward a healthy divorce, keeping the kids as a priority. This one action of doing everything in the kids' best interest has made the co-parenting relationship doable.

We informed the children about the divorce nine months after I told my former husband. I hate the term "ex." It sounds so severe and lacking transition. Two days after telling the kids, to move from being husband and wife to being co-parents, we did a closing ceremony on our marriage. We wrote a Co-Parenting Oath to replace the oath my husband had written for me when he proposed.

We burned the former oath, put the new oath in a frame and our wedding rings back in the box. Closing the lid on the ring box reminded me of a casket closing.

The co-parenting oath now hangs in both the Mom House and the Dad House.

We are a family even with two homes. Neither home is broken. The kids continue to be happy free spirits and know they are loved and supported.

And even though I was leaving for a life that was right for me, it was also very hard to look at the first family portrait minus me. It was a picture of the kids and their dad taken at his church. It hangs in the Dad House. There is nothing wrong with this new family portrait, it was just another uncomfortable moment to get through so I could move forward.

As I came out to my friends one by one, many saw me as an ally and confidante. My married friends started to share with me crazy events, frustrations and emotions going on in their marriages.

The summer after coming out, I noticed I was having an overwhelming urge to hold babies. Any baby, strangers' babies—it didn't matter. Even though I'd experienced having three of my own, I just wanted to go up to people and say, "Let me hold your baby. I know you don't know me, but trust me. It's okay, really."

I asked my therapist what was going on with all this baby holding. She said, "It's you wanting to hold your little self, to finally love yourself and give yourself what you deserve." Well, I'm past my stranger-with-baby stalking phase, but I do recognize more often that I AM taking care of myself by making decisions that honor me.

Self-love is an amazing awareness. It's being able to look into a mirror and into your own eyes and say, "I love you," without an ounce of doubt causing you to clench. Self-love is being okay with the choices and decisions you make for yourself. Self-love is not going quietly to your room when you have a conflicting opinion with a family member. Self-love is walking away from self-consciousness and being "ready to rock" whatever room I enter.

Self-love shows up in my relationships with other people. While writing this book, my father passed away and my Mom's dementia picked up the pace. Self-love allows me to accept her exactly where she is in her life without clinging to the idea that she needs to regain her clarity AND BE A CERTAIN WAY FOR ME. I just accept her as she is. Self-love makes it easy for me to make sure she is in a happy, loving community during her process of leaving.

The Diane and   Co-Parenting Oath
Sunday, January 27, 2008

We promise to see Claire, Adam, and Sophie as the first priority in our evolving relationship.

We promise to base all our decisions with Claire's, Adam's, and Sophie's best interests at heart.

We promise to keep God in our hearts.

With Love and kindness we promise to be the best co-parents we can be.

We promise to live our lives with open hearts.

We promise that everything that we give to this family comes from the best that is in us.

We promise to work together from this day forward and leave the past in the past.

We promise to always treat each other with honesty, respect, and dignity.

We promise to be able to inspire the kids as much as they inspire us.

We promise to be seekers of personal growth.

We promise that all five of us will help each other live to our truest fullest potential.

You were born to love, no matter the cost, no matter what someone else said, and no matter how the past once played out. -TUT "Notes from the Universe"

Unfolding

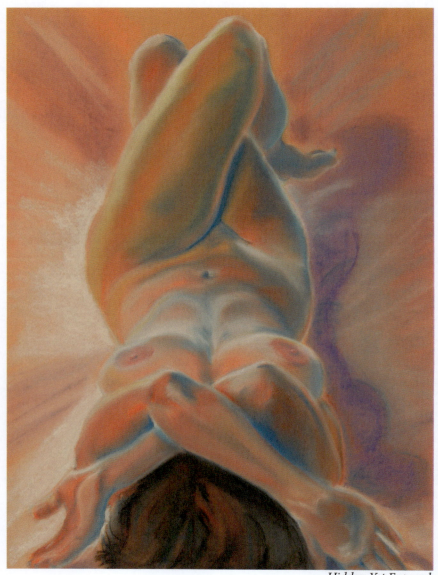

Hidden Yet Exposed

Chapter 9
Full circle

During MY AWAKENING, I've reconnected back to art. My work is no longer about holding it up and wanting a positive response but more of a self-study. Before personal growth, I avoided looking at myself inside and out. I hated mirrors and cameras. Now, when someone brings a camera out, I'm ready to say cheese :)

I used to believe I was very unappealing. Someone else would be a better choice—for anything.

On this healing/life journey, at some point I got the idea to draw myself. I began a series of self-studies that forced me to look at myself for hours at a time. I must say how grateful I am to a couple of drawing instructors I met along the way. The first had amazing teaching ability to hone and guide her students' talents and potential. And the second (who was very talented in his own right, but not a very hands-on or even very stay-in-the-classroom-during-class type), forced me to be my own motivator to greater creativity.

The following is my artist statement about these drawings seen through out this book:

I turned my focus to my own Personal Healing Art Process. The life I was leading before was one of secrets. Everything about myself was false. I couldn't bear to look at myself inside or out. So I began drawing a series of nudes. I took the idea of having nothing to hide and combined it with my passion for drawing the human figure. I chose poses that represent my secretive past, my uninhibited present, and my honesty about the future.

This work is an exploration of my personal transformation from secrets to freedom. From closed to open. From fear to love. These sketches tell the story of me coming out of a conventional, suburban lifestyle and literally coming out as a gay person. I have fought my sexual orientation my whole life. I have kept my true identity hidden, which I believe has kept all my passions and talents hidden as well. Everything about me is coming out.

These pieces demonstrate myself emerging both as an artist, and even more importantly, as a human being. I believe these personal sketches demonstrate the truth of the statement: Vulnerability exhibits our strengths. My artwork has never been stronger!

I believe my work is also very timely. It reflects the same massive awakening occurring on our planet today. People are awakening to love instead of fear. People are searching for truth, honesty and love.

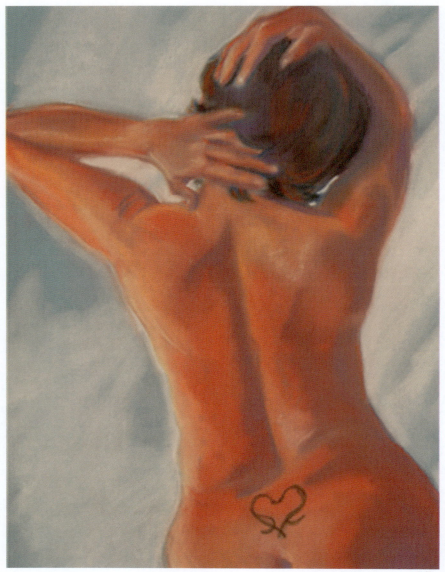

Holla

Chapter 9
Choices

I didn't choose to be gay, but for a long time—too long —I tried to choose not to be gay. It didn't work, and I was at a point where trying to be someone and something I'm not, I found my face aging rapidly and my hair falling out. During my life, I was never suicidal, but I would think how much easier it would be not "to be," how time and space were just fine before February 25, 1965.

Sometimes while watching a fatal tragedy on TV, I would wonder if there was anyone on board the fallen airplane or in the burning building that was just set free from their life of hiding.

Recently, while falling asleep, I realized I had gotten myself to a place where I feel safe and happy—a place that honors me both physically and emotionally.
I no longer cling to Fridays or dread Mondays. I don't live for the weekend or need the weather to be sunny and 70. I stopped creating countdown calendars to upcoming vacations and never do I try to get a day, a week or a

month "over with." I LIVE every day. I live every day in Love—in Love with myself and in Love with life.

I also am aware of help all around me. If I really listen, there are positive messages everywhere. Just the other day a cycling instructor offered this advice during class, "Don't drop your head. It cuts off your airway. You can't breathe and you won't have the strength to continue." How true, I thought to myself.

Head up! Be Proud! Breathe . . .

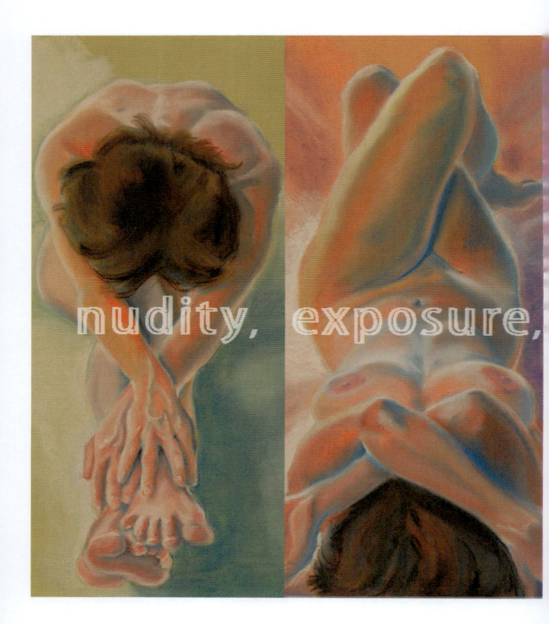